Inventions Help People

by Stanley Brown

Editorial Offices: Glenview, Illinois • Parsippany, New Jersey • New York, New York
Sales Offices: Needham, Massachusetts • Duluth, Georgia • Glenview, Illinois
Coppell, Texas • Sacramento, California • Mesa, Arizona

writing

washing

cooking

Inventors look carefully at the way people do things. Inventors can observe for hours how people write, cook, wash clothes, clean the house, or wash the car. Then an inventor may come up with an idea to make the job easier. An inventor may invent a machine that helps people.

washboard

washing machine

Let's think about washing clothes. For many years, people could wash clothes only by hand. They used washboards to clean their clothes. Their hands hurt after doing the wash. It was hard work!

Then about 100 years ago, the first electric washing machine was invented. Washing machines made the job easier!

Let's look at writing. For many years, people had to write by hand. At home or at school, people wrote letters, notes, or reports. They did it all by hand! Your hand got tired if you had to write many letters! If you used a pen and ink, your hands could get dirty! Or, your paper could get an ink spot.

typewriter

About 140 years ago, the typewriter was invented. It made putting words on paper faster and easier.

Many people still like to write letters and cards by hand. It makes the letters and the cards very special.

Before there were cars, people walked, rode horses, or took trains to get places. The first car was made more than 120 years ago. The first cars were very slow. Later, new inventions made the car faster.

car

A car can make going from place to place faster. When there is a lot of traffic, it is not always faster. A lot of people still like to walk to a store or other places. Walking can be healthy and fun! It is a good way to exercise.

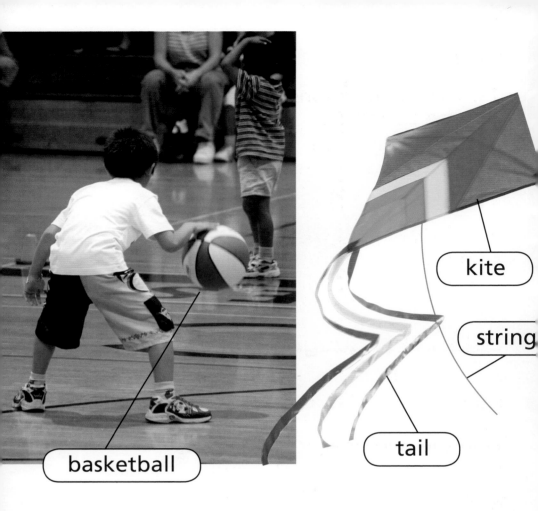

basketball

kite

string

tail

Some inventions are for fun.

About 115 years ago, the game of basketball was invented. This helped people play a sport in the winter.

Here is a very old invention: the kite. It was invented about 3,000 years ago! Aren't kites fun?

What would you like to invent?